Welcome to and Table Talk

Exploring the Bible together to discover God's Rescue Plan

CW00348454

XTB

XTB stands for **eXplore The Bible**.

Read a bit of the Bible each day.
Unpack Christmas with the help of Dr. Luke.
Find out all about God's Rescue Plan.

Are you ready to explore the Bible? Fill in the bookmark...
...then turn over the page to start exploring with XTB!

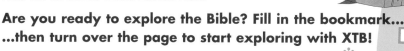

Table Talk FOR FAMILIES

Table Talk helps children and adults explore the Bible together. It can be used by:

- Families
- One adult with one child
- Children's leaders with their groups
- Any other way you want to try

Table Talk uses the same Bible passages as XTB so that they can be used together if wanted. Table Talk is at the back of this book. It's easy to spot because it's printed sideways!

Never done anything like this before? Write to us or call for a free fact sheet (details opposite) or check out our website (www.thegoodbook.co.uk).

I am .... (Age)

My birthday is

....

My favourite chocolate bar is

....

My favourite Christmas song is

....

OLD TESTAMENT	NEW TESTAMENT
Genesis	Matthew
Exodus	Mark
Leviticus	**Luke**
Numbers	John
Deuteronomy	Acts
Joshua	Romans
Judges	1 Corinthians
Ruth	2 Corinthians
1 Samuel	Galatians
2 Samuel	Ephesians
1 Kings	Philippians
2 Kings	Colossians
1 Chronicles	1 Thessalonians
2 Chronicles	2 Thessalonians
Ezra	1 Timothy
Nehemiah	2 Timothy
Esther	Titus
Job	Philemon
Psalms	Hebrews
Proverbs	James
Ecclesiastes	1 Peter
Song of Solomon	2 Peter
Isaiah	1 John
Jeremiah	2 John
Lamentations	3 John
Ezekiel	Jude
Daniel	Revelation
Hosea	
Joel	
Amos	
Obadiah	
Jonah	
Micah	
Nahum	
Habakkuk	
Zephaniah	
Haggai	
Zechariah	
Malachi	

How to find your way around the Bible

Look out for the READ sign.
It tells you what Bible bit to read.

READ
Luke 2v11

So, if the notes say... READ Luke 2v11
...this means chapter 2 and verse 11
...and this is how you find it.

Use the **Contents** page in your Bible to find where Luke begins

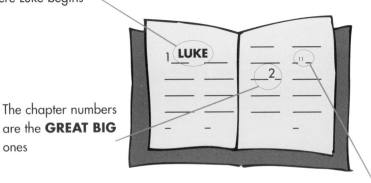

The chapter numbers are the **GREAT BIG** ones

The verse numbers are the tiny ones!

Oops! Keep getting lost?
Cut out this bookmark and use it to keep your place.

How to use xtb

1  Find a time and place when you can read the Bible each day.

2  Get your Bible, a pencil and your XTB notes.

3  Ask God to help you to understand what you read.

4  Read today's XTB page and Bible bit.

5  Pray about what you have read and learnt.

6  If you can, talk to an adult about what you've learnt. Remind them about **Table Talk** at the back of this book.

Rescue! stickers

This Christmas pack comes with free Rescue! stickers. Be ready to stick one in every time Luke tells us something about God's Rescue Plan.

(If your stickers are missing, contact us at the address inside the front cover and we'll send you some more.)

Are you ready to find out about **God's Rescue Plan?**
Stick your first sticker here, then hurry on to Day 1.

DAY 1 RESCUE NOT REINDEER

Circle the pictures that remind you of Christmas.

You probably didn't circle the fire engine or the helicopter. But surprisingly they have loads more to do with Christmas than reindeer or snowmen!
That's because Christmas is about being rescued.

READ
Luke 2v11

An angel said this to some shepherds on the night Jesus was born. *Fill in the gaps.*

Your **S**...................
was born - **C**...............
the **L**...........

God's Rescue Plan

The first part of the Bible (the Old Testament) shows that people are in trouble. They need to be rescued. God promised that He would send a Rescuer (Saviour), called the Messiah or Christ.

Meet Dr. Luke

We're going to find out about God's Rescue Plan with the help of Dr. Luke. (You can discover more about Luke on the back page of this book.)

Luke wrote his book (called Luke's Gospel) to show **WHO** the Rescuer is and **WHY** we need rescuing. Luke shows us that **Jesus** is the promised Rescuer.

PRAY

Dear God, please help me to learn more about your Rescue Plan as I read Luke's book.
Amen

DAY 2 CHECK IT OUT!

The school Christmas tree gets knocked over. Three people saw what happened, but your teacher doesn't ask them. He just assumes it was Clumsy Chris, and makes him stay in to fix it.

FAIR or UNFAIR?

....

READ Luke 1v1-4

Like that unfair teacher, some people make their minds up about Jesus without looking at the evidence (proof). Luke wants us to be **sure of the facts**. That's why he wrote his book.

Follow the lines to check the evidence Luke used for his book.

A Spoken reports from eye-witnesses who saw Jesus themselves

B Written reports

C Luke's own careful investigation

verse 1

verse 2

verse 3

Who was Theophilus?
We don't know! The name Theophilus means "friend of God". He was someone who wanted to know more about Jesus. Luke also wrote **Acts** for Theophilus. Friends of God want to know all about Jesus.

Do you?

PRAY

Ask God to help you to know more about Jesus as you read about Him in Luke's book.

Answers: A-v2, B-v1, C-v3

Dr. Luke starts the Christmas story by introducing us to some people who lived 2000 years ago.

READ
Luke 1v5-7

Underline the right words:

Zechariah was a **doctor/priest/king** and Elizabeth was his **wife/mother/sister**. They both **ignored/forgot/obeyed** God. They were **old/young** and had **2/3/no** children.

Take the first letter of each picture:

They _ _ _ _ _ God.

They _ _ _ _ _ _ _ God.

It was Zechariah's turn to be on duty in the Temple. While he was there something very surprising happened.

READ
Luke 1v11

Who did Zechariah see?

The angel is called Gabriel. He has a mess from God. **More about that tomorrow**

Can you think of someone else Gabriel gave a message to at Christmas time? **M** ___
Check Luke 1v27 if you're not sure.
More about that on Day 6.

THINK + PRAY

Look at verse 6 again. Do you want to love and obey God like Zechariah and Elizabeth? Talk to God about your answer.

DAY 4 AND THE ANGEL SAID...

Perhaps you have a gran and grandad. Imagine they suddenly announce that they are going to have a baby! **What would you think?**

No way!

They're joking!

When Gabriel suddenly appeared in the temple he had an amazing message for Zechariah and Elizabeth.

READ Luke 1v11-14

Gabriel told Zechariah that he and Elizabeth would have a son. What would the baby be called?

J _ _ _

Who would be full of joy because of John's birth?
- Zechariah
- Elizabeth
- and ....(v14)

CHRISTMAS CLUE
100s of years before, God promised to send a messenger to His people, to tell them "Get ready for the Rescuer". When John grew up he would be that messenger.

xtb Luke 1v11-17

He will get the Lord's people ready for him. (v17)

God kept His promise by sending John as His messenger. John's birth was all part of God's Rescue Plan. **Stick a Rescue! sticker here.**

RESCUE!

God has made many promises in the Bible. **How many will He keep?**

PRAY

God kept His promise to send John as the messenger. Thank God for always keeping His promises.

DAY 5 WOULD YOU BELIEVE IT?

I DON'T BELIEVE IT!

Which of these would you believe?

- The planet Jupiter is made of chocolate. ✔ ✘
- All schools are being closed down for ever. ✔ ✘
- Your mum will be the next Queen of England. ✔ ✘

Zechariah knew that his wife Elizabeth wasn't able to have children. But the angel Gabriel has just told him that she will have a son. **Do you think he will believe the angel?**

Yes / No / Maybe

ZECHARIAH

READ Luke 1v18-20

Did Zechariah believe the angel?
Yes / No
The angel told him, "Because you have not believed, you will be unable to s_____ until the day the promise comes true." (v20)

ELIZABETH

READ Luke 1v23-25

The name John means **"Gift of God"**.
Elizabeth knew that her son was from G_____ (v25)

God doesn't usually send angels to speak to us! Instead, God speaks to us when we read His word in the Bible.

THINK + PRAY

Is it easy to believe the Bible?

Is it easy to do what it says?

Ask God to help you to understand, believe and obey what you read in the Bible.

DAY 6 HAPPY FAMILIES

READ
Luke 1v26-31

THE MOTHER

Jesus' mother lived in a small town called Nazareth, in the country of Israel. What was her name?

M _ _ _

Think Spot

Why do you think God sent **an angel** to tell Mary about her baby?

THE FATHER?

Mary was soon to marry a carpenter called Joseph, who came from the family line of King David.
But Joseph wasn't Jesus' father!

READ
Luke 1v32-33

Mary's son would be known as The S _ _ of the

M _ _ _   H _ _ _

 The Most High is another name for God. That means that God Himself was Jesus' Father!

THE SON

Gabriel told Mary that her son would be the most amazing baby ever born.

Jesus was **God's own Son**, who came to earth as a human baby!

More about Jesus, and why He came, tomorrow.

PRAY

As you look forward to Christmas, thank God for sending His Son, Jesus, as our best Christmas present ever.

WHO IS JESUS?

 Luke 1v30-33

READ
Luke 1v30-33

Today's verses tell us loads of great things about Jesus. Use the arrow code to check them out.

ARROW CODE

A = ⇧
B = ⬈
D = ⬊
E = ⇩
F = ⬈
G = ⇦
I = ⬆
K = ➡
N = ⬋
O = ⬅
R = ◁
S = ▷
T = ◁
V = △

The name **Jesus** means

_ _ _ _ _ _ _ _

It tells us who Jesus is
★ He is **G** _ _
It tells us what Jesus does
★ He **S** _ _ _ _
Time for another Rescue! sticker

RESCUE!

Jesus will be

_ _ _ _ _

The **Greatest Person** who has ever lived!

Jesus will be called the

_ _ _ _ _ _ _ _

As we saw yesterday, Jesus is **God's own Son**, born as a human baby.

Jesus will be

_ _ _ _ _ _ _ _ _ _ _

Jesus is still alive today, ruling as King. We can know Him as our friend and King.

THINK + PRAY

Look again at the answers to the code. Choose one to give thanks to God for.

DAY 8 MISSION IMPOSSIBLE?

The angel has just told Mary some stunning stuff about her son.
How do you think she felt?

Tick your answers and add more.

Worried

Amazed

Scared

Excited

2

READ
Luke 1v34-38

Gabriel told Mary that her son wouldn't have a human father.

He told her that **GOD** would be the father of her son, and reminded her that God can do **ANYTHING!**

3

Which of these words do you think are the most important?
Colour them in.

For nothing is impossible with God. (v37)

4 **MARY**
• **believed** what the angel said;
• **trusted** God to do what He said;
• was willing to **obey** God and do whatever He wanted.

THINK + PRAY

5 **YOU**
• do you **believe** what the Bible says?
• do you **trust** God's promises?
• are you willing to **obey** God and do whatever He wants?

6 Dear God, please help me to believe the Bible, trust Your promises and be ready to do whatever You want. Amen

DAY 9 JUMPING FOR JOY

Did you know that pregnant women sometimes feel their babies moving inside them? Before I was born, I kicked my mum so often she thought I was going to be a footballer!

In today's story, Elizabeth feels her baby jumping for joy inside her. Dr. Luke tells us why... [And it's nothing to do with football!]

READ
Luke 1v39-45

Did you know?

The Holy Spirit points people to Jesus.
That's how Elizabeth knew Mary was to be Jesus' mum.

The Holy Spirit hel us today too.
He helps us to underst the Bible as we read about Jesus.

Who came to visit Elizabeth? M _ _ _

Mary and Elizabeth were relatives. Mary hadn't had time to tell Elizabeth her news yet. So how did Elizabeth know? (v41)

She was filled with the

H _ _ _   S _ _ _ _ _

THINK + PRAY

Even though he was not yet born, Elizabeth's baby (John) jumped for joy because of Jesus. At Christmas time we celebrate th birth of Jesus in lots of differe ways. Can you think of some wa to show your joy toda

Can you - use your voice? (*praying, singing*..
- use your body? (*jumping, dancing*...)
- use your hands? (*drawing, making*...)
- think of something even better?

Choose one way now to say thank you to God for sending Jesus.

Match the songs with the pictures.
The first one is done for you.

1 Happy b _____ to you.

2 Rudolph the _____ reindeer.

3 Humpty _____ sat on a wall.

4 Magnificat anima mea Dominum.

You've probably never heard of Song 4
(*it's in latin!*), but it's been one of the most popular songs in churches for hundreds of years. Read it for yourself (in English!) to find out why...

READ
Luke 1v46-50

Mary was singing about God
• what God is like and
• what He has done.

Rescue! sticker

Mary said that God is... Add the missing letters
a, e, i, o + y

S _ v _ o u r   h _ l _ (v49)
(v47)

RESCUE!

m _ g h t _   full of
(v49)   m _ r c _ (v50)

It's quite a long song. If you have time, read the rest (v 51-55) to see what else Mary praises God for.

PRAY

What can **you** praise God for?
Add your own ideas to this prayer.

I praise you God because
_____

and I thank you because
_____

Amen

DAY 11 LOOK WHO'S TALKING!

1 Do you remember God's promises to Zechariah and Elizabeth?

READ
Luke 1v57

Check days 4 & 5 if you're not sure.

God said Elizabeth would have a son. **SHE DID!**

2

READ
Luke 1v59-63

• What did Elizabeth call her son? (v60) _____

• What did Zechariah call him? (v63) _____

God said their son was to be called John. **HE WAS!**

GOD IS IN CHARGE

3 Zechariah hadn't spoken a word for nine months. Speechless!
Why? - because he hadn't believed what the angel told him about Elizabeth having a son.

READ
Luke 1v64

God said Zechariah would start speaking again after the baby was born. **HE DID!**

4 John grew up to do a special job for God. He told people how to get ready for Jesus the rescuer. Just as **God said!**

THINK + PRAY

When God says that something will happen - it does! How does this make you feel? Talk to God about it.

DAY 12 MESSAGE MATTERS

 Luke 1v67-75

Unjumble the letters to find five kinds of message:

- this message comes by post
- a telephone message
- a message on a computer
- a holiday message
- a Christmas message

treelt	L_____
enohp llac	P_____ C____
aeilm	E_____
costdrap	P_____
drac	C_____

In today's reading, Zechariah gives another kind of message. A **prophecy** is a message from God. The first part of Zechariah's message is all about what God has done...

READ
Luke 1v67-71

> **Praise God. He has saved his people. (v68)**

Find all of these words in the wordsearch. The first one is done for you.

```
G P R A I S E G O D
O D S E H E H A S N
T J E S A V E D S U
S T O R E H I S S C
P E O P L E U E U S
```

The word **"message"** appears **12** times on this page. **Can you find them all?**

Copy the left over letters from the wordsearch (in order) to find the secret message:

_ _ _ _ _ _

_ _ _ _ _ _ _

_ _ _ _ _ _ _ _

Stick a Rescue! sticker here. RESCUE!

PRAY

> *Dear God, thank you for keeping your promise to send Jesus to rescue us.*

Answers: letter, phone call, email, postcard, card

DAY 13 GOD'S RESCUE PLAN

Spot the difference. There are six to find.

You'd need a super-speedy rescue in a fire. **God's Rescue Plan** saves us from something even worse. Read the second part of Zechariah's prophecy to see **WHY** we need rescuing...

READ
Luke 1v76-77

Zechariah says that his son John will be God's messenger, telling people to get ready to be rescued.

How will people be saved?

By having their
s_____ f_____ (v77)

SIN is a **h-u-g-e** problem. To discover more about how we can be rescued from it turn to **The Sin Solution** on the next page.

Stick a Rescue! sticker here.

RESCUE!

Time to think

John's job was to tell people about Jesus the Rescuer.

- Have you been rescued by Jesus?
- Do you want to be?
  (Go back to The Sin Solution if you're not sure.)
- Do you want to tell your friends about Jesus?

PRAY

Talk to Jesus about your answers. Ask Him to help you.

THE SIN SOLUTION

We know that Jesus is the Rescuer but **WHY** do we need rescuing?

WHAT IS SIN?

We all like to be in charge of our own lives. We do what **we** want, instead of what **God** wants. This is called Sin.

For example, when we tell lies or don't share with others.

WHAT DOES SIN DO?

Sin separates us from God. It stops us from knowing Him and stops us being His friends. The final result of sin is death. You can see why we need a Rescuer!

HOW DOES JESUS RESCUE US?

Jesus didn't stay a baby. When He was about 33 years old, Jesus was crucified. He was nailed to a cross and left to die.

As He died all the sins of the world (all the wrongs people had done) were put onto Jesus. He took all of our sin onto Himself, taking the punishment we deserve. He died in our place, as our Rescuer, so that we can be forgiven.

When Jesus died, He dealt with the problem of sin. That means that there is nothing to separate us from God any more. That's great news for you and me! **And there's more...**

WHAT HAPPENED NEXT?

Jesus died on the cross as our Rescuer - but He didn't stay dead! After three days God brought Him back to life. Jesus is still alive today, ruling as King.

Is Jesus your Rescuer, Friend and King? **Turn to the next page to find out...**

AM I A CHRISTIAN?

Not sure if you're a Christian? Then check it out below...

Christians are people who have been rescued by Jesus and follow Him as their King.

> **You can't become a Christian by trying to be good.**

That's great news, since you can't be totally good all the time!

It's about accepting what Jesus did on the cross to rescue you. To do that, you will need to **ABCD**.

A **Admit** your sin - that you do, say and think wrong things. Tell God you are sorry. Ask Him to forgive you, and to help you to change. There will be some wrong things you have to stop doing.

B **Believe** that Jesus died for you, to take the punishment for your sin; that He came back to life, and that He is still alive today.

C **Consider** the cost of living like God's friend from now on, with Him in charge. It won't be easy. Ask God to help you do this.

D **Do** something about it! In the past you've gone your own way rather than God's way. Will you hand control of your life over to Him from now on? If you're ready to ABCD, then talk to God now. This prayer will help you.

> Dear God,
> I have done and said and thought things that are wrong. I am really sorry. Please forgive me. Thank you for sending Jesus to die for me. From now on, please help me to live as one of Your friends, with You in charge. Amen

Jesus welcomes everyone who comes to Him. If you have put your trust in Him, He has rescued you from your sins and will help you to live for Him. That's great news!

ONCE IN ROYAL DAVID'S CITY Luke 2v1-7

SILLY CENSUS

Name?
Age?
Pets?
Pairs of wellies?
Pairs of green socks?
Chocolate eaten today?

The Roman Census wasn't about green socks! They wanted to know all about the people living in the Roman Empire - to work out how much money (tax!) they must pay to Rome.

READ
Luke 2v1-7

WOW!
God's son has been born. The Rescuer who came to save the world!

Did you know?
A manger is an animal's food box!

Born in
B_____(v6)

No room at
_____(v7)

Wrapped in
_____(v7)

Name?
J_____

NOT what people expected (no crown or rich robes) but this was the promised **Rescuer** - born to save us.

Stick a Rescue! sticker here.

 RESCUE!

PRAY

Dear God, thank you for keeping your promise to send Jesus to rescue us.

DAY 15 TERRIFYING AND TERRIFIC

 Luke 2v8-14

What are you scared of...?
[*Tick the boxes*]

	NO PROBLEM!	ER...	AAAGH!
• SPIDERS	☐	☐	☐
• SNAKES	☐	☐	☐
• THE DARK	☐	☐	☐
• ANGELS	☐	☐	☐

Did you tick "No problem!" for angels?
Surprisingly, every time someone meets an angel in the Bible they're terrified! The first thing the angel has to say is, "Don't be afraid."

READ
Luke 2v8-14

This scary angel had terrific news...

Use these words: people joy good great news

> G_____ N_____ of G_____ J_____
> for all the **P_____** (v10)

2000 years ago the angel brought **Good News** about the birth of the **Saviour**. The message was for **ALL** the people—this means you and me as well!

Stick a Rescue! sticker he

RESCU

THINK + PRAY

Why is Jesus' birth Good News for you? Thank God for sending Jesus as your Saviour.

DAY 16 SHEPHERDS' DELIGHT

 **xtb** Luke 2v15-20

READ
Luke 2v15-16

What did the shepherds do when the angels had gone?

 _____

_____

How can **you** find out more about Jesus? Circle the words that will help you, and add more of your own.

TV

Bible

football

prayer

church

chocolate

READ
Luke 2v17-18

The shepherds told others what the angel had said about Jesus. Who can **you** tell about Jesus this week?

 _____

READ
Luke 2v19-20

How much was **true** of what the shepherds had been told?
[*Tick your answer*]

some

all

How much is **true** of what you have read about Jesus in the Bible? [*Tick your answer*]

all

some

PRAY

Look again at the name you wrote above. Ask God to help you to tell that person about Jesus this week.

DAY 17 KING FOR EVER

What's your name?

Do you know what it means?

 Lots of names have meanings. **Paul** means "little", **Sarah** means "princess" and **Mark** means "large hammer"!!

Do you remember what **Jesus** means?

G_____ **S**_____

[*Check Day 7 if you're not sure*]

READ
Luke 2v21

Who gave Jesus His name?(v21)

_____

Jesus is often called **Jesus Christ** - but Christ isn't His surname. He wasn't called Mr Christ! CHRIST is a title. *Take the first letter of each picture to find out what it means.*

_ _ _ _ _ _   _ _ _ _ _ _ _ _   _ _ _ _ _

CHRISTMAS

- is when we celebrate the coming of Jesus as our **KING**.

CHRISTIANS

- are people who follow Jesus as their **KING**.

Are **you** a Christian? _____
If you're not sure, turn to "Am I a Christian?" opposite Day 14 to find out more.

 Dr. Luke's second book - called **Acts** - is all about the first Christians. Sometimes it was very dangerous to be a Christian - they were whipped, put in prison or fed to lions! They needed God's help to keep following King Jesus - no matter what happened.

PRAY

Ask God to help you to obey Jesus as your King, even when it's hard.

DAY 18 SING-ALONG-A-SIMEON

Joseph and **Mary** went to the temple in **Jerusalem** to give thanks to God for Jesus. **Simeon** was an old man who was waiting for God to keep His **promise** to save His people. The Holy **Spirit** had told Simeon that he wouldn't die until he had seen the promised **Rescuer** for himself.

Fit the underlined words into the crossword.

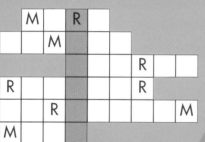

Rescue! sticker

RESCUE!

Simeon didn't live in the temple, (*unlike Anna who we meet tomorrow*), so the Holy Spirit made sure he was there at the right time to meet Mary and Joseph...

READ Luke 2v27-33

Jesus is only one week old. He doesn't look like a King or a powerful Rescuer - but He is!

As soon as Simeon saw Jesus, he knew that God had kept His promise at last.

Copy verse 30 here

In verse 32 Simeon says that Jesus has come to rescue Gentiles (non-Jews) as well as Jews. That's **everyone everywhere** - even you and me!

THINK + PRAY

When Simeon met Jesus he thanked God in a song. How will you show God that you are thankful for Jesus?

DAY 19 ANNA'S RESCUE RECIPE

xtb Luke 2v36-38

READ
Luke 2v36-38

Anna is very old. She has waited all her life to see God's promised Rescuer.

Draw her face when she sees Jesus.

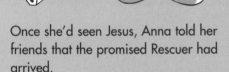

Once she'd seen Jesus, Anna told her friends that the promised Rescuer had arrived.

Stick a Rescue! sticker here.

RESCUE!

Have you spotted how often I write about the Rescuer?

Count up how many Rescue! stickers you've stuck in so far. **Don't forget to check the first few pages!**

How many stickers are there?

Check your answer below.

"Anna never left the Temple; day and night she worshipped God, fasting and praying." (v37)
[**Fasting** = going without food]

Underline three things that show that Anna loved God.

Think of three things **you** can do to show that you love God.

1

2

3

PRAY

Look again at your list above. Ask God to help you to do these things.

DAY 20 WAITING, WAITING, WAITING

W-a-i-t-i-n-g for Christmas takes ages! What do you find hardest to wait for?

Draw or write your answers here.

...meon and Anna had **waited and ...aited** for God to send the Rescuer. ...ow at last He's arrived. Read the end of ...apter two to see what happened to Jesus ...ext...

READ Luke 2v39-40

Jesus grew up in

N_____ (v39)

People had to **wait** another 30 years before Jesus started to travel around Israel telling them about **God's Rescue Plan.**

The great news for us today is that we don't have to **wait** at all.

- Jesus the Rescuer has come.
- The Bible tells us all about Him.
- He is alive and with us today.

WOW!

What are some of the things you have learnt about Jesus from Dr. Luke?
[See Day 7 if you want help.]

_____

_____

_____

_____

PRAY

Dear God, I want to thank you for sending Jesus because

_____

_____

Our Christmas special ends with a story about a rescue. We've whizzed forward 30 years. Jesus has now grown up. He told this story to help people understand **who** He came to rescue.

READ
Luke 15v1-7

Imagine a shepherd losing a sheep and saying "I don't care"!

What does the shepherd in the story do when he loses his sheep?

Jesus loves you **loads more** than any shepherd. You are **so special** to Him that He died to rescue you from your sins!

This man welcomes sinners! (v2)

The religious leaders were always amazed at the kind of people Jesus chose to rescue.

Circle the people Jesus doesn't care about...

very old   rich   sick   young

smelly   naughty

poor   rude

"That's right! Jesus cares about EVERYONE."

Read verse 7 again
This means that the angels have a party when someone is rescued by Jesus!

If **you** have been rescued by Jesus - they had a party for you!!

WOW!

RESCUE!

PRAY

Dear Jesus, thank you that you love me so much that you died to rescue me. Please help me to follow you always. Amen

WELCOME TO TABLE TALK

The aim of this section is to help you to read the Bible together as a family. Each day provides a short family Bible time which, with your own adaptation, could work for ages 4 to 10. We've included some optional follow on material linked with the XTB children's notes, which take the passage further for 7-10s.

TABLE TALK

A short family Bible time for daily use. Table Talk takes about five minutes, maybe at breakfast, or after an evening meal. Choose whatever time and place suits you best as a family.

Table Talk includes a simple discussion starter or activity that leads into a short Bible reading. This is followed by a few questions and a suggestion for prayer.

Table Talk can be used on its own, or alongside the XTB children's notes.

BUILDING UP

The Building Up section of the family pack is designed to link up with XTB children's notes. After your child has worked through XTB on their own, the questions in Building Up can be used to build on what they have learnt. Questions may reinforce the main teaching point, stretch your child's understanding or develop how the passage applies to us today.

Building Up can also be used as an extra question section to add to those in Table Talk. This may be particularly valuable if you have older children.

xtb

XTB Bible reading notes for children are based on the same passages from Luke as Table Talk. XTB notes can be used on their own, or with Table Talk.

Suggestions for using XTB and Table Talk:

★ The family do **Table Talk** together at breakfast. Older children do **XTB** on their own later, then share what they've learnt with a parent using **Building Up**.
★ **Or:** Children use **XTB** notes on their own.
★ **Or:** Children's leaders use **XTB** and **Table Talk** to read the Bible with their group.
★ **Or:** Some or all of the family use **Table Talk** as the basis for a short family time, with added questions from the **Building Up** section when appropriate.

DAY 1 — RESCUE NOT REINDEER

Today's passages are:
Table Talk : Luke 2v11
XTB : Luke 2v11

TABLE TALK

DO (*You need pen & paper.*) Write **RESCUE** in the middle of the paper. Brainstorm together (say whatever comes into your brain) about the word Rescue. (*e.g. Who rescues us? What from?*) Write (*or draw!*) everyone's ideas on the paper.

READ Christmas is all about being **Rescued**. Read what an angel told some shepherds on the night that Jesus was born. **Read Luke 2v11**

TALK What names did the angel give to Jesus? (*Saviour, Christ, Lord*) Which of these names means Rescuer? The angel is saying that Christmas is about being Rescued and that Jesus is the Rescuer. This is **God's Rescue Plan** for the world.

DO Add "Jesus" and "Christmas" to your paper - and draw Jesus in the manger. Stick it on the wall.

PRAY Ask God to help you learn more about His Rescue Plan this Christmas.

> **BUILDING UP**
> Today's **XTB** notes show that Christmas is about being rescued.
>
> Ask your child what Christmas is about. Did it surprise them to find that Christmas is about being rescued? Why/why not? Ask them to explain the

DAY 2 — CHECK IT OUT!

Today's passages are:
Table Talk : Luke 1v4
XTB : Luke 1v1-4

TABLE TALK

Quick Quiz: Ask each person to say one thing about Jesus. These questions may help to start you off.

- At Christmas we remember a special baby being born. Who is he?
- What was his mum's name?
- Who was Jesus' father?
- What town was Jesus born in?

READ Sometimes people have muddled ideas about Jesus, or don't know much about Him. Luke wrote his book to help us be sure of the **truth**. **Read Luke 1v4**

DO (*optional*) Read about Dr. Luke on the back page of this book.

TALK Dr. Luke's book will help us learn more about Jesus. How else can we learn about Jesus? (e.g. Church, Bible club, other Christians.)

PRAY Ask God to help you learn more about Jesus this Christmas.

> **BUILDING UP**
> The main theme of **XTB** today is that Luke carefully investigated his book because he wants us to know the truth about Jesus.
>
> Ask what your child has learnt about Luke. Luke checked his facts carefully. Does it matter that we know the **truth** about Jesus, rather than made up stories?

DAY 3 WHO'S WHO IN THE RESCUE?

Today's passages are:
Table Talk : Luke 1v6-7
XTB : Luke 1v5-11

TABLE TALK

(optional) Everyone draw a quick picture (1 minute) of a man and woman in Bible clothing. **(Stick figures are fine! - Use the pictures for the story.)**

Dr. Luke starts the Christmas story by telling us about Zechariah and his wife Elizabeth, who lived 2000 years ago. **Read Luke 1v6-7**

Zechariah & Elizabeth don't know it yet but they're going to be part of God's Rescue Plan for the world. What does Luke tell us about them? (*Very old, no children, they loved and obeyed God.*)

Is it easy to obey God? - at home, school, work... (*It's important that adults are honest about this too.*) What can help us to obey God?

Ask God to help you to love and obey Him like Zechariah and Elizabeth did.

BUILDING UP
In today's **XTB** notes we meet a couple who love and obey God. They're about to be part of God's Rescue Plan.

Ask what your child has learnt about Zechariah and Elizabeth. Do they want to love and obey God like Zechariah & Elizabeth? What makes it hard?

DAY 4 Notes for Parents

Why start with John?

If we were writing Jesus' life story we would probably start with His birth. Instead, Luke starts with the birth of Jesus' cousin John. Why?

In the Old Testament, as well as promises about the coming Rescuer (the Christ/Messiah) there are promises that God will send a **messenger** first. This messenger will tell people to get ready for the Rescuer.

John the Baptist was the messenger. He was a part of God's Rescue Plan, preparing people for the coming Rescuer. Matthew explains it like this:

> *John was the man the prophet Isaiah was talking about when he said, "Someone is shouting in the desert, 'Prepare a road for the Lord; make a straight path for him to travel!'" Matthew 3v3*

The promised messenger would be like the prophet Elijah. He is mentioned in the last two verses of the Old Testament (Malachi 4v5-6) where "he will bring fathers and children together again". Gabriel quotes this in his message to John's father Zechariah (Luke 1v17).

Older children: might like to research some of these promises for themselves, to see how God's Rescue Plan was coming together. A good start would be to compare Matthew 3v1-3 with Malachi 3v1 and Isaiah 40v3. This is then summed up in the words Zechariah spoke when John was born (Luke 1v76-77).

The theme of John as messenger is also mentioned on Days 10-12.

DAY 4 AND THE ANGEL SAID...

Today's passages are:
Table Talk : Luke 1v13-14
XTB : Luke 1v11-17

TABLE TALK

Talk about anyone you know who is going to have a baby soon. When is the baby due? Have they chosen a name? How do they feel?

Zechariah & Elizabeth have never been able to have children, and now they're very old. But God sends an angel to give Zechariah an amazing message. **Read Luke 1v13-14**

What did the angel promise? Who chose the baby's name? (*God did - the angel was sent by God.*) Do you think God kept His promise? Why?

When John grew up he became God's messenger, telling people all about Jesus. Pray for people who tell you (and others) about Jesus.

*Please see **Notes for Parents** on the previous page for further suggestions based on today's passage.*

BUILDING UP
In today's **XTB** notes Gabriel announces the coming birth of John - God's promised messenger who will prepare people for the Rescuer.

Please see Notes for Parents on the previous page for suggestions for how to follow up today's

DAY 5 WOULD YOU BELIEVE IT?

Today's passages are:
Table Talk : Luke 1v19-20
XTB : Luke 1v18-25

TABLE TALK

Pretend there's an elephant in your garden, or that Mummy has turned into a goat! Does your child believe you? Why / why not?

The angel had been sent by God to tell Zechariah that Elizabeth would have a baby, but Zechariah found it **very hard** to believe. **Read Luke 1v19-20**

What was the angel's name? Did Zechariah believe his message? What did the angel say would happen to Zechariah? (*He wouldn't speak a word until John was born.*)

God doesn't usually send angels to speak to us! God speaks to us when we read His word - the Bible. Ask God to help you to understand and believe what the Bible says.

BUILDING UP
Today's **XTB** notes ask if we believe God's promises to us in the Bible, or doubt Him as Zechariah did.

Ask what your child learnt about Zechariah. Why do they think he doubted the angel's message? Why do we sometimes doubt God's promises to us? (*Be ready to be honest about your own doubts too.*) What can help us to trust God?

DAY 6-8 Notes for Parents

Making a display

Children often understand and remember things better when they have something to look at. The next three days include suggestions for a simple display (just three sheets of paper) to help them remember what they have learnt about Jesus. The display could look like this:

Jesus is the Son of God

Jesus - God saves

Nothing is impossible with God

If older children have the use of a computer they might like to design these three sheets as a project.

Who is Jesus' father?

On Days 5,6 & 7, Table Talk and XTB both focus on who Jesus' father is. This may need to be handled sensitively with some children. Mary was soon to marry Joseph, who would look after Jesus as He grew up. But Joseph wasn't Jesus' father - **God is!** The Bible makes it clear that Mary was a virgin when she became pregnant. (See Luke 1v34-37).

Luke was a doctor. He knew the 'impossibility' of a virgin birth. He recorded it because it was the truth - one of many facts about Jesus that was first promised 100s of years earlier. Matthew explains it like this:

Now all this happened in order to make what the Lord had said through the prophet come true. "A virgin will become pregnant and have a son, and he will be called Immanuel" (which means, 'God is

DAY 6 HAPPY FAMILIES

Today's passages are:
Table Talk : Luke 1v30-31
XTB : Luke 1v26-33

TABLE TALK

Talk about any family likenesses in your family. Do you look the same? (*e.g. hair, eyes*) Do you like or hate the same things? (*e.g. sprouts!*)

 READ
God sent the angel Gabriel to visit a young woman called Mary. Read part of his message in **Lk 1v30-31**

 TALK
What did Gabriel tell Mary? Mary was going to be Jesus' mum, but who was His father? (*God - not Joseph! v35*) When Jesus grew up He was exactly like His Father - God. Can you think of examples? (*e.g. He loved everyone, did miracles, came to rescue us...*)

 DO
(*Optional - see Notes for Parents opposite.*) Write **"Jesus is the Son of God"** on a large sheet of paper. Stick it on the wall.

 PRAY
Thank God for sending His Son to be born as a human baby.

BUILDING UP
The main point of **XTB** today is that Jesus was God's own Son, who came to earth as a human baby.

Ask what your child has learnt about Jesus. **XTB** describes Jesus as "our best Christmas present ever". What do they think this means? Do they

DAY 7   WHO IS JESUS?

Today's passages are:
Table Talk : Luke 1v31-32
XTB : Luke 1v30-33

TABLE TALK

Talk about your names. Who chose each person's name? Why did they choose that name?

READ We're still looking at Gabriel's message to Mary. Read part of it in **Luke 1v31-32**

TALK Who chose the name **Jesus**? In Bible times names were often chosen because of their meaning. The name Jesus means "God saves". Why is this a good name for Him? (*Because His name helps us to remember who Jesus is [God] and what He does [saves].*)

DO (*optional*) Write the words **"Jesus - God saves"** on a large sheet of paper. Stick it on the wall as a reminder. (*Please see **Notes for Parents** for Days 6-8 on previous page*)

PRAY Thank God for sending Jesus to save us.

BUILDING UP
XTB today looks at four facts about Jesus. He is the Son of God; He saves us; He is great; He is King for ever.

Ask your child what the four answers were in XTB's secret code. What does it mean for us today that

DAY 8   MISSION IMPOSSIBLE?

Today's passages are:
Table Talk : Luke 1v37
XTB : Luke 1v34-38

TABLE TALK

REMEMBER 1: Ask everyone what they have learnt about Jesus so far. (*The display should help.*)

REMEMBER 2: Can they remember what the angel told Mary?

READ Mary was told some amazing things about her son. She asked how all of this was possible. Gabriel told Mary that **God** would be the Father of her son - and then reminded her of an important fact about God... **Read Luke 1v37**

DO (*optional*) Write the words **"Nothing is impossible with God"** to add to your display. (*Copy v37 from your own Bible version if it uses different words.*)

REMEMBER 3: Learn v37 together as a memory verse. Agree to test each other during the day.

PRAY Thank God that He can do ANYTHING.

BUILDING UP
Today's **XTB** notes show that "nothing is impossible with God" - not even a virgin birth!

Ask your child what they have learnt about God. Does this make it easier to trust Him and do what He wants? Why / why not?

DAY 9 JUMPING FOR JOY!

> Today's passages are:
> **Table Talk** : Luke 1v44-45
> **XTB** : Luke 1v39-45

TABLE TALK

If you're a mum, talk about what it felt like to have a baby inside you. Did he/she ever kick?

Mary went to see her relatives Zechariah and Elizabeth. Read what Elizabeth said to Mary when she arrived. **Read Luke 1v44-45**

What did Elizabeth's baby (John) do? Why were Elizabeth (& John!) so happy? (*Jesus had come.*)

DO Even though he wasn't yet born, John **jumped for joy** because of Jesus. Together think of some ways you could show your joy today. (*Suggestions: Sing a song, draw a picture, write a thankyou prayer - and add it to the display.*)
Agree to do something together later if there isn't time now.

PRAY Use one of your ideas to thank God for sending Jesus.

BUILDING UP
In today's **XTB** notes we see how the not-yet-born John the Baptist jumps for joy when Mary visits Elizabeth.

Ask your child to tell you about Mary's visit to Elizabeth. What happened and why? Why do they think John was so excited? (*Maybe link this to his future job as God's messenger: see **Notes for***

DAY 10 MARY'S SONG

> Today's passages are:
> **Table Talk**: Luke 1v46-47
> **XTB**: Luke 1v46-56

TABLE TALK

Talk about your favourite choruses or Christmas carols. Or play one on a tape for everyone to listen to (or even sing along!).

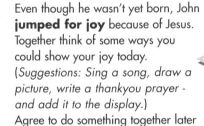

READ Mary is still with Elizabeth. She sings a song of praise to God. **Read Luke 1v46-47**

TALK Who is Mary singing about? What two names does she give to God? (*Lord, God my Saviour*) The rest of Mary's song describes what God is **like** and what He has **done**.

DO Brainstorm a list of things you can praise and thank God for - what He is **like** and what He has **done**. (*Suggestion: If you write them down, you could add your list to the wall display.*)

PRAY Use your list to praise and thank God together.

BUILDING UP
XTB looks today at Mary's song of praise to God.

Ask your child what they learnt about God from Mary's song. If you have time read the rest of the song together (Luke 1v51-55). Choose one idea from the song to praise God for together.

DAY 11 LOOK WHO'S TALKING!

Today's passages are:
Table Talk : Luke 1v63-64
XTB : Luke 1v57-66

TABLE TALK

Try talking to each other <u>without</u> speaking (e.g. tell everyone one thing you did yesterday - but using **signs** or **actions**, not your **voice**!)

Remind each other of the story of Zechariah and Elizabeth:

- The angel Gabriel said they would have a son.
- Zechariah didn't believe, so he hasn't spoken for nine months!
- Now Elizabeth's baby has been born and they need to give him a name. **Read Luke 1v63-64**

What name did Zechariah write down? Now that he can speak again what does Zechariah start talking about? (*He starts praising God.*) What do you think Zechariah has learnt about God?

Like Zechariah we sometimes let God down or don't trust Him. Say sorry, and then thank God that He NEVER lets **us** down.

BUILDING UP
The main point of **XTB** today is that when God says that something will happen - it does!

Ask your child what they learnt about God from this story. Zechariah hadn't believed the angel, but God still kept His promise. Why?

DAY 12 MESSAGE MATTERS

Today's passages are:
Table Talk: Luke 1v68-69
XTB: Luke 1v67-75

TABLE TALK

Tom says "**I might** bring you a present", Sara says "**I'll try** to bring a present" and Tim says "**I promise...** to bring you a present." Who is most likely to bring the present?

100s of years earlier God had **promised** to send Jesus as the Rescuer, and John as the messenger. Now John's father Zechariah is praising God for what He has done... **Read Luke 1v68-69**

What does Zechariah say that God has done? (*Note: "redeemed" [NIV] = bought back or set free.*) Zechariah is talking about God's Rescue Plan. How has God kept His promise to rescue His people? (*By sending Jesus to be the Rescuer.*)

Tomorrow we will see **how** Jesus rescues us. Today, thank God for keeping His promise to send Jesus as our Rescuer.

BUILDING UP
Today's **XTB** notes look at Zechariah's prophecy when John is born. He praises God for saving His people.

Ask your child what they learnt from Zechariah's message. What was today's Rescue! sticker for?

The Book Illustration

This is a simple and effective way of explaining how Jesus died to rescue us. Use any book (*except a Bible, because the book stands for our sin!*)

Hold up your right hand. Explain that your hand represents you, and that the ceiling stands for God. Show the book, and ask them to imagine that it contains a record of your sin - every time you have done, said or thought things that are wrong. Put the book flat on your right hand.

Ask: "What does the book do?"

It separates you from God. This is a picture of what sin does. It gets in the way between us and God, and stops us knowing Him as our Friend.

Now hold up your left hand. This stands for Jesus. Explain that Jesus lived a perfect life. He never sinned. There was nothing separating Jesus from God.

Explain that as Jesus died on the cross, the sin of the whole world was put onto Him. Transfer the book from your right hand to your left hand to show this.

Ask: "What is there between Jesus and God?"

This is why Jesus died - to take the punishment for all our sin.

Now look back at your right hand.

Ask: "What is there between me and God?"

The answer is - Nothing!

When Jesus died on the cross, He took the punishment for our sin so that we can be forgiven. This means that there is nothing to separate us from God any more. This was **God's Rescue Plan** for us.

DAY 13 GOD'S RESCUE PLAN

Today's passages are:
Table Talk : Luke 1v76-77
XTB : Luke 1v76-80

TABLE TALK

When John grew up he told people about Jesus. List some of the people who tell **you** about Jesus.

 Read the next part of Zechariah's prophecy to see what John would do. **Read Luke 1v76-77**

 John told people they would be saved. How? (*v77 - by having their sins forgiven.*)

 Use the book illustration (*see **Notes for Parents** on this page*) to show how Jesus rescues us from our sins **and/or** read **The Sin Solution** together (opposite Day 13 of **XTB**).

Do you all understand how Jesus rescues us? If not, who could help explain it to you?

PRAY Pray for the people who tell you about Jesus. If possible, tell them you have prayed for them.

BUILDING UP

The theme of today's **XTB** notes is that the Rescuer has been sent to save people from their sins.

Ask what your child has learnt about God's Rescue Plan. Use the book illustration to reinforce this - *see Notes for Parents* - or ask them to show you if they already

DAY 14 ONCE IN ROYAL DAVID'S CITY

Today's passages are:
Table Talk: Luke 2v6-7
XTB: Luke 2v1-7

TABLE TALK

Fill in a Census for your family - Name, Age, Favourite food (or dinosaur!), One thing you hate...

The Roman Census meant that Joseph and Mary went to Bethlehem - exactly where God said the Rescuer would be born!
Read Luke 2v6-7

(optional) Read Micah 5v2 for God's promise about Bethlehem.

What did Mary wrap her baby in? Why didn't she use disposable nappies? (Wrapping babies in strips of cloth was normal at that time - sleeping in mangers wasn't!) Jesus didn't **look** special - sleeping in an animal's food box! How do we know that He was?

PRAY Thank God that Jesus was born in Bethlehem, just as God said.

BUILDING UP
In **XTB** we focus on the birth of Jesus - who came as God's promised Rescuer.

Christmas is a celebration of something that happened 2000 years ago. Ask your child to imagine a friend asking them why we still celebrate Christmas today. What would they say?

DAY 15 TERRIFYING AND TERRIFIC

Today's passages are:
Table Talk : Luke 2v10-12
XTB : Luke 2v8-14

TABLE TALK

Talk about shepherds. What do they do to look after their sheep? Why would they stay with their sheep at night?

On the same night that Jesus was born, an angel appeared to some shepherds near Bethlehem. He had a thrilling message for them. **Read Luke 2v10-12**

What was the angel's message? How would the shepherds recognise the baby? The angel said that Jesus' birth was Good News for 'all the people'(v10). Who does that include? (Everyone **then**, everyone **now**, **You!**) Why is Jesus' birth Good News for you?

PRAY The angels then sang a song of praise to God. Pray (or sing!) your praise to God for sending Jesus as your Saviour.

BUILDING UP
Today's **XTB** notes look at why the angel's message about Jesus is Good News for ALL people.

Ask what your child learnt about angels. The final question in today's **XTB** notes is "Why is Jesus' birth Good News for you?" Ask your child what their answer was - and why.

DAY 16 SHEPHERDS' DELIGHT

Today's passages are:
Table Talk: Luke 2v16-18
XTB: Luke 2v15-20

TABLE TALK

Have you ever gone to visit a new-born baby? Where did you go? How did you know the baby had been born?

The angels had told the shepherds how to find Jesus, so after the angels left, they went into Bethlehem to see Jesus for themselves. **Read Lk 2v16-18**

What did the shepherds **see**? What did the shepherds **say**? (v17) The shepherds told other people about Jesus. Think of a way that you could tell someone about Jesus this week. (*Could you ...invite them to a Christmas service? ...send a card with a Christmas message? ...tell them what you've learnt doing Table Talk?...*)

Ask God to help you tell someone about Jesus this week.

BUILDING UP

In today's **XTB** notes we see how the shepherds find out about Jesus for themselves and then tell others about Him.

Ask your child who they could tell about Jesus. Talk together about some ways that they could tell this person about Jesus. Pray together, asking God for His help.

DAY 17 Notes for Parents

Names for Jesus - background information

In Bible times the meanings of names were often important. The names and titles for Jesus help us to understand who He is and why He came.

JESUS

The name Jesus means 'God Saves'. It reminds us who He is (God) and what He does (He saves).

IMMANUEL

Immanuel means "God with us". 600 years before Jesus was born, Isaiah prophesied that a virgin would have a son called Immanuel. See Isaiah 7v14 - also quoted in Matthew 1v22-23.

CHRIST

Christ (*Greek*) and **Messiah** (*Hebrew*) are the same name. The literal translation is 'the Anointed One'. A helpful way to understand this title is as 'God's Chosen King'. (For example, David was anointed with oil when God chose him as King of Israel - see 1 Samuel 16v13).

The first followers of Jesus were called **Christians** as a nickname - because they believed that Jesus was the promised King (the Christ).

Circumcision (v21)

Jewish boys were circumcised (a small piece of skin cut off from their penis) when they were eight days old. This was a reminder of God's covenant promises to His people. (Genesis 17v11-12)

DAY 17 KING FOR EVER

Today's passages are:
Table Talk : Luke 2v21
XTB : Luke 2v21

TABLE TALK

Make up some fun job titles - like Bob the Builder. (e.g. D____ the doctor, T_____ the train-driver, L____ the lion-tamer...)

Jesus was named when He was eight days old. **Read Luke 2v21** *See Notes for Parents for more details.*

Who first gave Jesus His name? (*The angel - who was told the name by God.*) Do you remember what the name **Jesus** means from Day 7? (*'God saves'*)

Jesus is also called **Christ**. This isn't His surname - it's a job description - like Bob the Builder! It means 'God's chosen King'. Christians are people who follow Jesus as King. What do you think it means for Jesus to be King of your life? (*He's in charge of your life, He looks after you, you need to obey Him...*)

Ask God to help you obey Jesus as King, even when it's hard.

BUILDING UP
The main point of **XTB** today is that Jesus is God's chosen King.

Ask your child what 'Christ' means. Ask what they think it means to have Jesus as their King. Are **they** ~~following King Jesus? Are you?~~

DAY 18 SING-ALONG-A-SIMEON

Today's passages are:
Table Talk: Luke 2v27-29
XTB: Luke 2v22-35

TABLE TALK

What things do parents do to show their thankfulness for a new baby?

Mary & Joseph went to the temple in Jerusalem to give thanks to God for Jesus.

Simeon was an old man who was waiting for God to send the promised Rescuer. God had promised that Simeon wouldn't die until he had seen the Rescuer for himself. **Read Luke 2v27-29**

Did God keep His promise to Simeon? Where did Simeon meet Jesus? The Bible promises that we can meet Jesus for ourselves too. Does God keep this promise? How?

When Simeon met Jesus he thanked God in a song. Give thanks to God that you have met Jesus too.

BUILDING UP
In today's **XTB** notes Simeon thanks God for keeping His promise to send Jesus the Rescuer.

Ask your child what they have learnt about Simeon. Look at Luke 2v32. Simeon says here that Jesus has come to rescue Gentiles (non-Jews) as well as Jews. Thank God that this includes **everyone** - even you!

DAY 19 ANNA'S RESCUE RECIPE

Today's passages are:
Table Talk : Luke 2v38
XTB : Luke 2v36-38

TABLE TALK

Brainstorm a list of places where people can live. (*e.g. house, tent, boat, caravan, on the streets...*)

 Anna was a very old lady who lived in the **temple**. She had waited all her life to see God's promised Rescuer. **Read Luke 2v38**

 How do you think Anna felt when she saw Jesus? Luke tells us that Anna thanked God. What do you think she thanked Him for? What can **you** thank God for today? (*It may help to write a list.*)

 (*optional*) Read the end of v37 which lists what Anna did in the temple. How can we tell that Anna loved God? What can you do to show that **you** love God? How can you help each other do this today?

 Use your list to say Thank You to God.

BUILDING UP
The theme of **XTB** today is Anna's love for God. The notes ask how we can be like her.

Ask what your child has learnt about Anna. What three things did they list to show that they love God? Talk about how you can help each other to do these things.

DAY 20 WAITING, WAITING, WAITING

Today's passages are:
Table Talk: Luke 2v39-40
XTB: Luke 2v39-40

TABLE TALK

Where were you each born?
Did you grow up there, or move away?

 Jesus was born in Bethlehem, but He didn't grow up there. **Read Luke 2v39-40**

 Where did Jesus grow up?

 (*optional*) Use a Bible map (*in your Bible?*) to find Bethlehem and Jerusalem (in the South) and Nazareth (North). What happened in each place? (Luke 2v7; v22; v39)

 People now had to wait 30 years before Jesus began travelling through Israel telling them about God's Rescue Plan. What does v40 tell us about how Jesus grew up? How can **we** grow to be more like Jesus? (*Children and adults.*)

PRAY **Ask God to help you to grow more like Jesus.**

BUILDING UP
Today's **XTB** notes show that people waited a long time for Jesus - but that we don't have to wait at all.

Ask what your child has learnt about Jesus from Dr. Luke's Gospel. Thank God that we don't need to wait to learn about Jesus - the Bible tells us all we need

DAY 21 JESUS LOVES RESCUING YOU!

Today's passages are:
Table Talk : Luke 15v4-6
XTB : Luke 15v1-7

TABLE TALK
Think of some Bible rescue stories. (*If needed give clues for Crossing the Red Sea, Joshua & the walls of Jericho, Jesus calming the storm...*)

READ We've whizzed forward 30 years to a rescue story Jesus told about a lost sheep. **Read Luke 15v4-6**

TALK How many sheep did the shepherd have? What did he do when he lost one? What did he do when he found his lost sheep?

Verse 7 tells us what happens when a lost person is rescued by Jesus - the angels in heaven have a party! Have the angels had a party for each of you? (*They have if you've asked Jesus to rescue you from your sins.*) If you're not sure, check **The Sin Solution** opposite Day 13 of **XTB.**

PRAY **Thank Jesus that He loves you so much that He died for you.**

BUILDING UP
Today's **XTB** notes show that Jesus loves rescuing us and is delighted when we put our faith in Him.

Ask your child does Jesus love them? How much? Thank Him that nothing we do will make Him love us any less (or more!) than He already does. (*But we should still want*

What Next?

Explore some more **Rescue Stories** from the Bible. Here are a few to start you off...

From Luke's Gospel
• Jesus calms a storm Luke 8v22-25
• Jesus heals a blind man Luke 18v35-43
• Zacchaeus meets Jesus Luke 19v1-10
• The thief on the cross Luke 23v32-43

From the rest of the Bible
• Crossing the red sea Exodus 14v13-22
• The fiery furnace Daniel 3v16-28
• Jairus' daughter Matthew 9v18-26
• Peter escapes prison Acts 12v6-17

OTHER BOOKS TO HELP YOU...
Look out for **Easter Unscrambled** (unpack Easter with the help of Dr. Luke), and **Summer Signposts** (find out more about who Jesus is and why He came by following the signposts in John's Gospel).

XTB and **Table Talk** are also available in 12 undated issues to help children and families explore the Bible together. Available from your local Christian bookshop—or call us on 0845 225 0880 or visit www.thegoodbook.co.uk to order a copy.